African Wild Dogs

An Educational Children's Book about African Wild Dogs with Fun Facts & Photos

Abby Daniele

Abby Daniele

Copyright © 2016 by Abby Daniele

All rights reserved. No part of this book may be used or reproduced in any manner whatsoever without the express written permission of the publisher except for the use of brief quotations in a book review

Image Credits: Royalty free images reproduced under license from various stock image repositories. Under a creative commons licenses.

I am an African Wild Dog.

I have white, black and yellow fur.

African Wild Dogs

I have long legs and four toes on each foot.

My ears are big and round so I can hear far and wide.

I can give birth to six babies.

Both my mother and father takes care of me.

You can find me in Africa.

My name also means" painted-wolf" because I have black and white splotches on my body.

I share my food with other African Wild Dogs.

I like to eat meat.

I hunt food with other African Wild Dogs.

Me and my family usually help each other hunt down antelope and sometime buffalo.

I live in a very big neighborhood.

The entire Africa is my home.

I have a lot of friends.

I like to jump around and play with my friends.

I have a very strong bite.

I run very fast when I'm hunting.

We can also hear very well.

We sing when we're happy.

We also love to eat birds, rodents and small animals.

I have a lot of brothers and sisters.

Made in the USA
Middletown, DE
05 June 2017